COLLEGE BOUND

The Ultimate List of Conversations to Help Your Teen through High School

MELANIE PRATHER STUDER

This book is dedicated to Kent. Thanks for putting up with me writing as life continued around me!

Thanks to Ann for being a great partner in crime on

www.parentinghighschoolers.com

Finally, thanks to our three boys: Sam, Will, and Jake–Thanks for being our guinea pigs!

"Parents can only give good advice or put them on the right paths, but the final forming of a person's character lies in their own hands." -Anne Frank

CONTENTS

INTRODUCTION

Do you have teenagers? Do they want to go to college? Are you feeling overwhelmed with everything that you think that you need to know? Do you need a blueprint or a guide to help them through high school? This book will help you navigate high school with college as a goal. However, all the following conversations will help your teens whatever they decide to do.

If you answered yes to any of the above questions, or have even more questions than that, then you're in the right place.

I started writing this book, *College Bound* when my oldest was fifteen. Now, almost seven years later, we have two sons in college, and one in eighth grade.

My husband and I have learned a few things in the past few years, and I want to share these things with you so that you know what to expect as your teen starts high school. If your child is in middle school, even better, because you can get a head start on this process.

All the information that follows will help you and your teens on whatever path they decide to take. However, most of the information does pertain to college preparation.

You will learn from our experiences about ways to help your child make the most out of high school. Your teen will be prepared for college, trade school, the military or even the real world after reading *College Bound*.

TERMS TO KNOW

To get into the college game, you need to know the terminology.

COA—COST OF ATTENDANCE, THIS INCLUDES tuition and fees, also housing if you plan to live on campus, but not any other costs such as transportation, food, entertainment, and so on.

COCURRICULAR—RELATED BUT ONLY complementary to the official curriculum, as a civic or service activity outside the classroom. For instance, a church group would be a cocurricular activity. These will be activities to put on the high school resume.

DEFERMENT—PAYMENTS ON LOANS PAUSED UP TO three years. Subsidized interest is paid for by the federal government, and unsubsidized interest will accrue. Certain qualifications have to be met, and you have to apply for this.

This term can also be used to talk about deferring college for a gap year. This would mean putting college off for one year.

EFC—ESTIMATED FAMILY CONTRIBUTION—THIS is determined by filling out the FAFSA. It's the amount that the government thinks your family should be able to pay. Its exact definition is "a measure of your family's financial strength and is calculated according to a formula established by law." (I think we could live on rice and beans and maybe afford our EFC!)

EXTRACURRICULAR—OUTSIDE THE REGULAR curriculum or program of courses: football, orchestra, and so on. These activities from high school will be put on the high school resume. Any of these activities from college can be put on a resume as well.

FAFSA—FREE APPLICATION FOR FEDERAL Student Aid. The due date for filing is October 1 every year starting with your teen's senior year in high school. This will need to be completed every year through their senior year in college. If you have more than one child, then you'll need to fill it out for each child falling into this age range who's going to college.

The sooner you fill it out, the more aid you might qualify for. Some schools give you financial aid based on just filling it out regardless of whether you qualify for federal aid! Again, fill it out every year!

FINANCIAL AID—THERE ARE TWO TYPES. THE money you may or may not have to repay after college.

Type 1: grants and scholarships—aid you do *not* have to repay.

Type 2: loans—money you *do* have to repay. There are subsidized and unsubsidized loans. Know the difference!

DIRECT SUBSIDIZED LOANS—THESE ARE LOANS designed for low-income undergraduate students. The government pays the interest while the student is at least enrolled half time, or if you enter deferment or forbearance once it comes time to repay the loan. Generally, there is a grace period after the graduation of a few months.

DIRECT UNSUBSIDIZED LOANS—THESE ARE loans that aren't based on financial assistance. They're still offered by the federal government. Since they aren't based on need, borrowers are expected to pay back the loan in full, including interest that has accrued throughout your college years. The principal becomes due a few months after school, plus the interest.

FORBEARANCE—POSTPONING LOAN PAYMENTS for up to twelve months—interest will accrue for both subsidized and unsubsidized loans. You have to qualify.

FORGIVENESS—UNDER CERTAIN circumstances, the federal government will cancel part or all of an educational loan. There are very specific ways to qualify: perform volunteer work, perform military service, teach, or practice medicine in certain types of communities or other specific criteria.

GAP YEAR—THIS IS A YEAR OFF. TYPICALLY TAKEN between high school and college for many reasons: volunteering, working to make money toward college, an alternate academic program, a mental health break. This can take many forms, and some kids do take a class or two to ease into college. A gap year can also happen after college before getting a job.

NET PRICE—WHAT YOU ACTUALLY PAY FOR college, almost always less than the published price. *Always* ask if there is more money available. I spoke with a college admissions counselor. She compared the cost of college to the cost of a car. The list price is the amount they would like to get from you, but the amount can be adjusted for better grades, test scores, BSA Eagle award, and so on. Also, colleges do expect for students to ask for a better deal, so *ask* because you will never know otherwise.

TUITION—ONLY THE COST OF THE CLASSES YOU take. This doesn't include any other expenses.

WORK STUDY—FEDERAL PROGRAM DESIGNED TO help low-income students work part-time to help with school costs.

❧ 2 ❧
START THE CONVERSATION

Just ten years ago, our first son started middle school. My husband and I had so many questions. We knew nothing. It was almost like having a baby again, seriously. Our heads were spinning!

There were so many issues that we suddenly had to help our son deal with. He was now switching classes instead of staying in one classroom all day, should he have a cell phone or no cell phone, his preteen attitude, and shifting friendships, to name a few.

Once your child enters middle school, high school looms ahead a mere three years. What should you know to help your teen be ready for this next step? What are the important things? What can you do to plan? How can you counsel him or her to be ready for whatever comes next?

My husband and I have learned many things having gone through the high school years twice already.

We asked friends with older children. We read lots of articles and blog posts and books. We talked to the guidance counselors. Mostly, we **talked** to each other and with our boys about anything and everything that we felt that they needed to know or they had questions about.

MIDDLE SCHOOL AND HIGH SCHOOL ARE EACH challenging in their own ways.

Middle school is a great time for kids to practice being good students, try new things, and grow into their own skins. It's an awkward and stressful time. This is a time to let them experience new things, knowing that you have their backs.

Keep the lines of communication open. There will be lots of attitude! I don't care if you have a girl or a boy, fourteen is the worst! Every parent that I've come into contact with, when their kid is this age, is wondering, *Where did our once fairly pleasant kid go?*

Hang in there. Be loving, consistent, persistent, but not overbearing—I know: this is a hard line to figure out.

High school is challenging in many ways, as well. First, grades will now count if your child is headed to college. Even if your teen decides against college, their future employer will want a resume. It will be nice to have a higher GPA for that. Many times, our kids aren't prepared for the academic intensity of high school, so watch out for that.

Their social lives are huge at this stage in the game. They'll have big expectations for this time in their lives. Your teen may have seen movies that romanticize these years. Find out what they're expecting, both the good and the bad. Your job is to help them stay grounded and have a realistic picture of what's coming these next few years.

This means that you **need** to continue to keep the lines of communication open. I can assure you that many times, no matter the age of your teens, they'll *not* want to talk to you. That doesn't mean to stop trying. Just try different times, different ways. Don't stop!

How can parents help their kids during these years?

My husband and I learned, over time, that it takes a series of conversations to hash out details regarding most things. We have family meetings and one-on-one meetings with each boy usually once a month, or at least each grading period. This is about every six weeks. Our older two boys are now in college, so we meet with them over holiday break and at the beginning and end of summer break.

First jobs. Driving rules. Cell phone usage. Dating. Classes that they want to take versus what they need to take. Is college the next step? If yes, then where, and if no, then what? These are just a sampling of the many myriad conversations that need to occur. I detail how to manage this process as you read further.

Take notes at each meeting.

We learned this the hard way. The notes don't have to be formal, but write down basic things like the date that you met with your teen, any decision that's reached, and what was the tentative plan of action. Also, take note of any deadlines or topics to be discussed at the next meeting.

If you don't take notes, then there's no record of the discussion. Time will be wasted at the next meeting arguing over something that you already thought was decided! Trust me on this one!

COLLEGE BOUND IS SET UP AS CONVERSATIONS TO have with your teen.

Grab https://parentinghighschoolers.com/college-bound from our website, www.parentinghighschoolers.com

READ THE BOOK ALL THE WAY THROUGH FIRST. Then decide which order works for your family. There is no one "right" order! There are questions at the end of each chapter, and space for notes.

Many of these conversations lend themselves to more than one meeting. Some will naturally lead to other topics. The chapters are written in the order that worked for writing this book. It isn't the order in which our family conversations occurred, and many of them keep recurring!

This book will cover important things you will need to know for college prep or any other future plans.

College Bound gives suggestions for topics that need to be discussed over time, and hopefully long before your teen's senior year! (Yet, if that's where you are, then by all means, start talking!)

HAVING A CONVERSATION WITH YOUR TEEN

There are probably a million ways that you can facilitate this process. I'll outline how we have simplified our conversations over the years with our family.

First, set the expectation. Our kids know that every grading period, and maybe even more often, we'll be meeting with each of them to talk. As the time approaches, we get out calendars and set a date so that everyone is on the same page. We meet with each child separate from the others. (We do have many full-family meetings, but for the purposes of this book, we'll stick to the individual meetings.)

Second, we **always start the meetings with something positive.** We visit for a while in a casual way to break the ice. Since the child already knows about the meeting, it isn't a hassle to get started.

We usually have the meetings at home, actually in our master bedroom. My husband and I like to present a united front to the kids. Even if we end up disagreeing about something, this location is our home base, so if we need to send the kids out so we can discuss something, we're already in our own room.

Next, we bring up concerns. There might be a number of them, there might be only a few or none. It doesn't have to be something that they're necessarily doing wrong, but maybe something that's coming up that they need to put some extra thought into.

This is the more difficult part of the conversation. One reason we like to plan this ahead of time is so that my husband and I can be on the same page or already know where we'll agree to disagree or have already made a compromise. The kids don't need to see or hear this part.

There have been times of tears, yelling, and frustration. But the purpose of the meetings is to work together to find solutions to problems or strategies to move forward.

My husband and I try to never be the ones yelling, but honestly, it has happened. The main thing is, at that point, we've all agreed to take a break after apologizing, and we meet again later, in maybe a half hour. (We never schedule anything for the afternoon or evening of the meeting, so that if we do need to take a couple of breaks, the time is there.)

Some of the issues that have come up have been: low grades, bad attitude, scheduling issues, and chores. You name it—we've probably discussed it. As college approaches, we've talked about budgeting, spending money for them, grade expectations, and many other things.

The thing to remember is that the sky's the limit when it comes to what can be discussed. The kids know that they can bring up concerns and problems to us as well. We don't set the agenda in stone. We always leave time for what the individual child would like to discuss as well.

Some issues or problems are ongoing. Both good things and bad. Here are some examples.

With kids going to college, there are visits, applications, interviews, housing, scholarships, and myriad other things to talk about. With the real world looming for our almost senior in college, we have started talking about internships, graduation, possible postgraduate plans, and so on. Our youngest is getting ready to start high school in the fall. Conversations have already started about expectations we have for him once he gets there.

I now have a notebook for each boy. As we approach each meeting, I write down the things that my husband and I would like to cover. We look back over the notes from our last two or three meetings to see if there were any unresolved issues, or things that we want to follow up on. I add those to my list of what's to be discussed.

As the meeting starts, I note the date. I don't take superdetailed notes, but I try to keep track up upcoming dates and questions that need to be answered. I write down anything that the boys bring up so that we won't forget.

Many times after a meeting, I'll outline a plan for that particular boy to remember. It's usually not more than half a page, and I try to include a quote or verse that's meaningful to the situation. A lot of times I've found these notes later in their top desk drawer or taped up by their beds.

The main thing about these conversations is to have them. I know that there have been times that our boys have *not* wanted to meet with us because they knew their grades were bad or that something else was happening that wasn't good.

However, as bad as the middle of the meeting could get, by the time it was over—sometimes a couple of breaks later—we always ended the meeting in a positive way. This is very important, **always end on a good note.** Apologize again, if feelings got out of hand. Ask your children if they have anything more to say about anything and be ready to hear it.

These meetings have been held regularly since they were in grade school, and maybe even before. I didn't used to take notes. We just always wanted to check in with the boys in regular intervals.

We meet at those set times, but of course, things come up, and we'll randomly decide that we need to have a talk. It can be because of a discipline issue, a scheduling issue, or really anything. Because of the other scheduled meetings, I think that our boys are much more willing to talk with us since they know that we'll listen to them.

Even when they have gotten into trouble, they've always been able to talk with us about it, both at the time and later. Both of our older boys have told us more than once that their friends have been amazed by how much they're able to talk to us about anything and everything.

Talk with your kids, but also listen to them. If you let them, they'll tell you so much. They'll never tell you everything, but your relationship will be so much richer if you take the time to talk and listen to them regularly.

❧ 4 ❧
CONVERSATION #1
WHAT'S THE BIG DEAL?

Conversation #1 gives you information about why **all** the following conversations are so important. There are numbers and statistics that are really hard to believe. I share this information to make both you and your teen aware. This will help you both understand why all these conversations are so important as your child moves toward his or her future.

There are many reasons that families should be thinking about college and other future plans before high school. The biggest reason is *money*. Another reason to be thoughtful about all this is that your child's future will be greatly affected by the choices made today.

There are a variety of other reasons to be concerned. These were the two reasons at the top of our list when my oldest son was deciding on a college. Now we have two in college! Here are some astonishing facts.

Forty-five million students owe $1.56 *trillion* in

student debt as of February 4, 2019! (studentloan-hero.com)

This number is astronomical and growing every year. Make decisions about your child's college based on the amount of money that you have saved (or not). The choice of a major is also important. The likelihood of your child earning enough to make a decent living when college is finished is also very important.

Do some research into what your child is interested in. Have your teen do research as well. If your teen has no idea about what they would like to do in the future, then they should look up the careers that they're interested in.

Compare the training and schooling required for different careers, amount that they could make in those careers, and start making some decisions based on their findings.

Approximately 70 percent of graduates with bachelor's degrees leave school with some amount of debt.

If student loans must be taken out, then pay attention to the total amount. Parents may not normally pay much attention to this because they know their student will ultimately be responsible for the total amount owed after graduation.

This isn't reasonable or fair. Help your child to add up the numbers, so that he will know what to expect in the near future.

Take care to be honest with her about what you can and

cannot afford to pay for college from the very beginning. That's where the conversation needs to begin.

Don't wait until your student's senior year. The discussion should begin even before high school **if possible**. That way, you're both aware of all the facts before the college search begins. However, if you're reading this later in your child's high school years, then by all means, talk about this **now**.

Loan payments upon graduation can be more than rent payments.

This is a very depressing reality! Make sure to research and find out approximately what a starting level employee in your child's field of study will earn. It may not be enough money to live on when including monthly student loan payments.

It would be good to find someone who has recently graduated in the field that your child has chosen. Find out what they get on their paycheck.

Then a discussion can be had with your student, and you can help them make an informed decision regarding their future. Making a good choice at the beginning of college is crucial.

Plan to graduate in four years.

This will mean careful planning from the beginning of the freshman year in college. A plan must be made with an advisor because otherwise, extra and unneeded classes will be taken.

The advisor will know when certain prerequisites are offered so that your student will be on the right track. These classes can get tricky to fit in with just four years.

Another thing to remember is that twelve hours is considered full time, but fifteen a semester is needed to graduate in four years. That's the difference of one class a semester, which would be very easy to add into a schedule.

The cost of college skyrockets after the first four years.

This means that switching majors can be a financial setback if done after the sophomore year. Most of the time, estimated costs for colleges are based on a four year plan. Another year of college at most schools will either cost for that extra year or add to the student loan debt that the student has to take out.

The opportunity cost for another year of college instead of working for a student is $30,000-50,000 in lost wages. This is whether the fifth year is free or not. (Some colleges are now offering the fifth year as an enrichment year.)

In other words, your child should try their very best to graduate in four years.

College grads in 2001 earned 10% more than they do now.

This is because the cost of living has increased so much. Many items that were once much more affordable such as healthcare are no longer fitting into even a reasonable budget.

This can be super frustrating for today's graduates because how can they get ahead if they're already behind?

Two out of three students graduating today won't find an adequate job, meaning one that would pay for a *reasonable* living as well as enough extra for loan payments... This goes along with what was said earlier. The fewer loans that they have, the easier life will be moving forward.

More than two-thirds of student loan borrowers were surprised by some aspect of their loan.

In fact, approximately 50% of college freshman seriously underestimate the amount of their student loan amount. (Brown Center on Education Policy at Brookings-December 2014)

Be very careful when reading the fine print on the documents that the college provides. If we hadn't paid attention to our son's financial package information, we would have accepted a student loan for him. It was a loan that he would have had to pay back with interest at the end of college.

It was right there in black and white, but if I hadn't been checking through each section, I would have missed this line item. I now know to look for it each semester and draw a line through it.

Just because something is written down on the proposed tuition paperwork doesn't mean that you, the consumer, need to utilize it. Look everything over very carefully.

31% of students who dropped out of college referred to finances as a reason.

This could be because parents did not want to admit that they couldn't afford the college that their child wanted to attend.

Yes, it might be embarrassing to have to admit. But, it will be so much worse if your child has to drop out for financial reasons that they were unaware of in the first place.

Real life happens.

We had my husband's student loans to pay off. Then real life happened, as in, we had bills to pay... We don't have that much saved in the way of college funds for our boys, and they know that good grades etc. will really help with getting good financial packages from schools.

It has helped that we have been honest and realistic with our boys. They've made good choices based on what we could afford to pay. We have also been very upfront with them about the fact that they're in charge of all their spending money once they're in college.

[Our oldest son had a great resume and fairly high grades (just shy of a 3.5) coming out of high school. He is attending a small private school with lots of merit-based scholarship money. He stayed under our budgeted amount and has continued to apply for other scholarships along the way.

Our middle son did fine in high school, but he did not have the grades for any merit scholarships. He currently attends the local community college, which has a dual program with our state university.

This means that the classes at the community college are free (except for books)–because he took advantage of a high school scholarship program (Missouri A+). With the dual program, he is then able to take one three-hour class at the university and live on campus in a dorm-this part isn't free.

He is able to have a real freshman year experience on campus with this program.

He is also staying under our budget so far.]

About half of all college graduates are living paycheck to paycheck, and many have had to resort to living with parents or grandparents.

I think back to when I first graduated. I truly lived paycheck to paycheck. I paid a little more in rent than I should have, but I was in a safe neighborhood, and that was important to me living in a big city for the first time in my life.

I literally lived on about $1.00 a day after all my expenses were paid. I lived on pasta and tuna at night, and knew, to the ounce, how much salad I could put in my container to stay at less than $2.00 each day for lunch in the cafeteria.

I couldn't afford to buy enough groceries for both dinners and lunches. I ate a lot of oatmeal! I didn't even have any furniture and slept on an air mattress for months.

Here's my question... Are kids today willing to do that?

I came from a nice home with everything I needed as I was growing up. But, I was READY to grow up and move on. I'm not sure about today's young graduates when it comes time to move on. Parents make it really easy for them to stay home.

It was made very clear to me that once I graduated from college, I was off of my parents' payroll. This is a discussion that needs to occur with you and your teen. What are your expectations? Find out what your teen thinks as well. This is something that needs to be made very clear from the beginning.

Here's the thing. Getting a couple of roommates and striking it out on their own, even if they're super poor-- is probably the best thing that we can do for our kids. At the very least, help them out at first, but work out a plan with your child for how they'll gradually move out and off of your payroll.

I read a story the other day about mother giraffes.

As soon as her baby giraffe struggles to his feet, the mom knocks him down. The baby struggles up again. Mom knocks him down again. It happens again and again.

Are giraffe moms being mean? No. Because, guess what? Pretty soon the little guy gets stronger and stronger, and more and more sturdy. Then, suddenly, he can stand on his own with no struggling or wobbling. He has learned to get to his feet, and she has done her job by preparing him.

How likely is loan forgiveness?

Loan forgiveness is very rare. It's *not* something our kids should be counting on at all. Their plan needs to be to work, work, and work some more—maybe at a main job with two or three side hustles to get their loans paid down.

Cometfi.com says that the average time to pay back a four-year degree is almost twenty years. National student loan average is about $37,000.

There are specific programs for loan forgiveness, but many will not kick in until at least 120 payments have been made, this would equal to ten years of payment. There are programs for veterans, teachers, and those people with disabilities. Do the research with your students before they graduate from college to find out the details, and whether or not they'll qualify.

The real world is manageable, but our kids need to have a plan and be mentally strong and able to handle it by being prepared.

Don't let these numbers scare you!

Now is definitely the time to start the process of preparing your child to go to college to get a great education and graduate with little to *no* debt. Both you and your student need to get into the mindset that this is a challenge that **can** be met.

Be proactive. You and your child need to be on the same page or at least supportive of each other's efforts. Take the time to be informed. Do research.

You can start now wherever you are, however old your child is. The sooner, the better!

CONVERSATION #2

START EARLY—MIDDLE SCHOOL

Conversation #2 could make such a difference for your child's future. Start all these conversations as early as possible. The main thing is to just **start**, however old your teen is right now.

One thing that we learned with our oldest son is that this whole college process could (and probably should) be started in middle school. The young teen years are when our kids really start to think about all the possibilities for their futures. You will be at such an advantage over other families that aren't as prepared.

Just to start the thinking process is a huge step in the right direction.

Start talking with your teens about things that they like to do or are interested in or are good at. This is a great way to keep the lines of communication open with your child.

Be interested. Don't rule anything out at this point. Your children will take classes and find out that they really don't like chemistry or Spanish or whatever. They might learn that they love to cook or to solve algebraic equations. Let them find these things out.

Encourage your middle school child to give new experiences a try.

Middle school is a great time for your children to figure out what they like and dislike. Have discussions with them about what is working at school and what isn't.

Talk about why some classes are harder than others. Is it the content? Are they more comfortable in a science class than an English class? These conversations are great launching pads for discussions about future majors in college or even future jobs.

Parents, if your teen does anything, including, and especially, having conversations with you about their future, then you're all a big step ahead.

Grades don't count yet toward college admission, but your students need to be doing their best in their classes and trying different ways to study and prepare for tests. Your students need to start figuring out how to manage their time.

Encourage your child to try different clubs and sports to see what they like. He will be able to eliminate some things. She also might find some activities to love for a lifetime.

As you travel, drive by colleges.

Stop and walk around during a school day. It will be more motivating than you think for these younger kids to see what might be in store for them in the future. Visiting a college will give them a tangible goal. They'll see firsthand what the campus looks and feels like.

Middle school might seem really young for this experience, but your teen will soak it all in, and will surprise you with their questions and observations. Give it a try, and see how it goes.

Start all this when your child is younger.

I think one huge mistake people make is waiting until junior year of high school to start these conversations, when teens are super busy.

If you're just now reading this, and your child is a junior or senior, it's not too late, but your time is limited. So get started as soon as possible!

✤ 6 ✤

CONVERSATION #3

HAVE THE MONEY TALK WITH YOUR TEEN!

Conversation #3 is a tough one. You're going to have to be honest with your children. This isn't easy. Especially if you know that they aren't going to like what you have to say. My husband and I have been there, done that, twice so far. It wasn't fun either time. But the outcome has been good both times, eventually.

Money is a touchy subject. Many people don't talk about it. Ever. Not with their spouses. Not with their friends. Especially not with their kids!

This can be a mistake. Unless you're parents with bottomless pockets that you don't mind emptying regularly for your child's education, this discussion **must** take place. The earlier, the better!

This would mean starting when your kids are young, as in elementary school if possible. Talk about all the financial terms. Let them borrow money from you, but charge interest. This shows them how it works in the real world.

Show them graphs of how compound interest works and help them to make savings goals.

Of course, if you're reading this, you probably have older kids. It isn't too late. You can still have these conversations and maybe show them a loan you're paying off, maybe your car. Talk about the loan amount, what a down payment is, how interest works, and the importance of making regular payments. Talk about what would happen to the life of the loan if an extra payment were to be made. Help them to see real-world examples of what loans really are like.

We're a team with our boys. They know that we're paying for their tuition. Together, we worked out a plan for the rest of their college expenses. This has been a conversation that has taken place over many years with many adjustments and compromises.

Every family has a different story. Figure yours out and discuss it with your child. Once your teens know your stories, they're better prepared for their own futures.

Your children must know if there is money saved for their education.

If so, how much?

This might be a really difficult conversation. You might not have any saved. Even if you have really good jobs, sometimes life gets in the way of the best of intentions. Better to share this information with your child now while there's still time to make a difference!

The information from this discussion will help you each to know what's needed in order to help your children get into a college, if that's the plan.

Meet together now, parents and teens, and make a plan.

Can any money be saved between now and the time that your teen will go to college? Do some sacrifices need to be made now in order to make a difference?

Have your teen meet with his or her guidance counselor now. Let the counselor know the situation. They can help with making a plan for what comes next.

Should your teen take a gap year to work full time?

If your teen decides on a gap year, which is a year off between high school and college, have them make a plan for what will happen during that year to help them grow as a person: a class or two, a job, travel, and so on. Most colleges would recommend getting accepted, then deferring for a year. This way your teen has a plan and is working toward it.

Your teen can keep any scholarships they receive and still enter as a freshman when the time comes. Have your teen talk with their college, and let them know the situation. If the college can work with your family, they will.

The FAFSA can, and should, be filled out before senior year.

The FAFSA is the Free Application for Federal Student

Aid. It needs to be filled out starting October 1 of your child's senior year. The FAFSA is a tool used by the government to determine who qualifies for federal student aid. It's based mostly on income. Colleges will use the information to award their own scholarships and grants, so this isn't something avoid. There's a website. You can just Google FAFSA.

The FAFSA can be filled out as an estimate before the senior year. (FAFSA4caster) This is a good idea to see where your family is, as far as receiving any federal aid. The FAFSA needs to be filled out **every** year.

FAFSA—Fill this out beginning October 1 senior year. I recommend filling out the FAFSA4caster before senior year, so that you know what to expect.

There will be many questions on the FAFSA that need very specific and detailed answers, so have your tax returns ready. There is a direct link to the IRS from the FAFSA, but it doesn't always work. Have your tax returns nearby just in case.

Even if you think (know) you won't qualify for any federal aid, fill it out. Schools use this as a tool for awarding aid of other kinds as well. My son's school awards $1,000 just for filling it out! I think he is now grandfathered in on this grant.

The FAFSA will generate an EFC (Estimated Family Contribution). This is the number that the government thinks that you should be able to pay toward college.

The number we were given would work if my husband and I both worked full-time making massive amounts of money. All joking aside, the number you receive will probably not be an accurate estimate of what you can actually afford, so be ready.

Remember: it's been said that it truly doesn't matter where an undergraduate degree comes from, just that you got it!

If there's no money saved, and your family is starting from scratch, have your teen get busy with getting good grades, good ACT or SAT scores, and look for scholarships everywhere!

One final word on this topic. Your retirement savings are important. It's for **your** future. We aren't touching our savings to help our children. This is our choice.

Your choice might be different. If you can, talk to a financial advisor before making any of these decisions. Knowledge is power.

CONVERSATION #4

SET UP A BUDGET

Conversation #4 is more of a process. This will take some time. A budget is never perfect, and it often needs to change over time. The best thing to do with a budget is to get started now.

Talk about expectations and budget categories. There are lots of templates online if you go to Google or Pinterest. Choose one that appeals to you and try it.

Set up a budget with your teen.

This should be one of the first things to do after you read this book (or while you're reading it!). A budget is a tool that helps keep track of money and where it goes, and your teen needs to get used to this experience.

Once your teens have a budget set up, they can more easily keep track of their earnings and savings. Help them to set up all the categories of expenses* that they have now and will have in college and after. Try to think of everything that they'll need to spend money on while they're in college or when they're just getting started out in the real world if that's what happens after high school.

*Some categories for expenses are: long-term savings, rainy day savings, fun money, rent, utilities (electric, gas, water), food, clothing, phone, gas, car insurance, car payment, cable, internet, health insurance, gift money, and possibly educational loans.

This exercise is so important! It will help everyone to get on the same page.

Will you pay for some of their expenses?

It's best to decide this ahead of the conversation with your child. Even if you're going to pay for some things, you need to be clear on exactly what and exactly how much you'll spend.

If you're in a divorce situation, try to get money matters discussed with your ex prior to this conversation. The best-case scenario would be to meet together as a group, but understandably, this may not be possible.

Eventually, your teens will be responsible for their own expenses. It's better for them to know what things cost and not be surprised or overwhelmed later.

How long will you be willing to pay for these expenses? Will it be until your children graduate? Until they get a full-time job? Until they reach a certain age?

For instance, until your child is twenty-six, you can cover

their health insurance. Are you willing to do this? Health care today is very expensive.

Your children's first full-time jobs upon graduation may not have benefits. Will they be able to afford it on their own? What if they have student loans to pay back?

A great way to start working this out would be to figure out what you're willing to pay for once they graduate. Have your child gradually start paying you for one expense at a time. For instance, you may be getting a better deal on cell phone service for your family. Have your teen start paying you for his or her portion. Then add in their portion of car insurance. Build it out from there.

Of course, this assumes that your child gets a job upon graduation. It may take a while to find a full-time job. This isn't to say that they can't find something to do. They can wait tables, clean houses, nanny, or use their computer skills to work online providing a service.

If they move back home, this needs to be a requirement—first, that they'll pay you rent, and second, while looking for a permanent job, that they're doing something productive for many hours of the day.

Living within a budget is a challenge.

It takes dedication and sacrifice. It may be a new way of life for your teens. But if you help them do this while they're still at home, it will be so much easier later. Help them to make some good choices now while they're young, and they'll get ahead much faster in the future.

In 2006, the average yearly total at a four-year college for tuition was $12,796. For the same year, the same costs for a four-year private school were $30,367.

In 2018, the average yearly total costs at a four-year public institution are $20,770, and the costs at a four-year private college are $46,950.

There is a term for this—*cost of attendance* (COA). Note that these numbers have almost doubled in just twelve years!

Future Income for Your Teen

Middle-income families' earnings have stagnated over the past years. This means students are borrowing larger amounts to pay for college. With larger debt upon graduation, these students are having to choose to delay major life events such as marriage, having children, and buying a home.

A manageable amount of debt is described as that in which the total amount is less than the borrower's total annual income. Another way to say that it's manageable if it could be paid back in less than ten years. (*Money* magazine, 2016)

This is the last conversation about money. The rest of the conversations are more to do with high school itself. Money is the foundation for any future that your teen has. It's also the most difficult topic to discuss. Your teens should now have the why and the how of that percolating and swirling around in their heads.

8

CONVERSATION #5

GETTING A JOB!

Conversation #5 can be a challenging discussion as well. Many people have strong feelings about this topic. We have some friends who feel strongly that their teens should work through high school. Many others feel quite the opposite.

This is a situation that should be handled on an individual basis. Both of our boys worked each summer once they were fifteen. One of them was a lifeguard at the neighborhood pool. The other washed dishes at a local restaurant. They've both worked for an apartment complex, ripping out carpets, painting, and some basic maintenance jobs around the complexes.

One of our boys also worked through the spring of his senior year. His class schedule permitted this, and he really got a good feel for balancing both school and work.

Their goal was to have a minimum of $3,000 saved for their freshman year of college for spending money. Any extra would go toward their sophomore years, and they both continue to have part time jobs while in college.

Your teen should get a job.

There are many great reasons for your teen to get a job. There are multiple benefits they'll gain from employment. The obvious one is money, but there are so many soft skills that they'll learn from a job as well.

Once they have a job, encourage them to save as much as they can for the future. They should set up a Roth IRA. By the way, a Roth IRA can be set up at any time—there's no minimum age.

Decide together what amount they should keep from each paycheck for spending. They can save any extra earnings. Our boys save toward their spending money for the school year in a local account, but they also take a certain amount and put into their Roths. Talk to your accountant about what constitutes earnings.

Your teen should put savings into their Roths, as well as a regular savings account. They should also have some spending money, but they should try to spend as little as possible. Encourage them to make good choices.

This is a process. Be patient and know that this is a great tool for many conversations.

One of our sons loved having money all of a sudden when he started working. At the end of the summer, we tracked on his debit card what he had spent his money on. He had spent a lot on eating out.

Once he saw the numbers, he was really mad at himself. But he learned some things. Sometimes it takes seeing the amount in black-and-white to see the big picture.

(We took each of our older boys to our financial advisor their senior years in high school. This was very eye-opening for them. They saw our budget and long-term goals. This is all part of our process of being honest with them. They had many questions, but I think that it was good for them to see how we're taking care of our money.)

There are many options for part-time jobs.

Teens will have to be creative and persistent to find jobs. Many grocery stores hire fourteen-year-olds, others sixteen-year-olds. Babysitting, mowing lawns, cleaning houses, running errands, dishwashing, and bussing tables at restaurants—these are all ideas for getting started. Check with your state to see what the law is for hiring age where you live.

There are many ways to find jobs. Your teen needs to ask around. This is a good time to practice writing a resume with any work experience they may have had up until now. Babysitting siblings, yardwork, and working for grandparents or a neighbor are all ways to get references and a basic resume written.

As teens get older, there are other opportunities. Once your teen is old enough to drive, a lot more opportunities open up. Teens need to be willing to work. Getting a job is one thing. Keeping it is another.

Some Advice for Your Teen

Show up on time. Look **everyone** in the eye. Be respectful. Be willing to do extra work. Be willing to stay late if it's needed. Be willing to take constructive criticism. Ask the boss if he or she sees room for improvement. Your teen's attitude will be noticed and either appreciated or not. If not, they might end up without a job!

These are called soft skills, and they can be learned on a job. According to *Forbes*, the top two soft skills are problem solving and emotion control. Employers today are looking for evidence of this in work experience and letters of recommendation that past employers can provide about your teen.

Work can be interesting and fun. Chores should definitely be a part of their lives from a young age so that they can develop good work habits and the beginnings of these soft skills.

Encourage your teens to add a job into their lives. Yes, your teens are busy, but there are so many part-time jobs available. Time management is a hard thing to teach, but having a job will be a great way to figure out how it works.

The best thing, other than getting and keeping a job, is to plan what will be done with the money earned.

If Your Teen Is Reluctant or Opposed to Working

I have two ideas for this problem. Hopefully, one or both will work. First, make it clear that this is an expectation. If your child is already a teenager, then tell him or her that on his or her next birthday or "this next summer," he or she will need to get a job. Make it plain that you won't be financing their fun anymore, or at least not 100% of it. This may not go over well, but the experience is worth it. Don't cave.

Second, show them a chart of what compound interest is. This was what motivated our kids. They decided on an amount that they wanted to save by the time that they were each twenty-one in their Roth account. They're both really close to this amount.

Our oldest son is going to be twenty-two this summer. He will be a year late on his goal, but he's been living on his earnings at school, and it has just taken a bit longer for him. Our middle son will be nineteen in a few days, and he'll accomplish his goal ahead of time! They're both excited to continue to save for both short-term and long-term goals.

Okay, this chapter still had a little bit to do with money. But, we cannot talk about getting a job without talking about money a little bit. Hopefully, the other benefits of getting and keeping a job will resonate with your teen.

9

CONVERSATION #6

WHY GRADES MATTER

Conversation #6 is so important. Many teens just don't care about school. They're killing time until high school is over. The best way to "get out" successfully is to do well and get good grades. Most of the time this means paying attention, turning in everything on time, and studying for tests. This is a minimum of course, but every little bit helps.

Colleges need your student's GPA to determine acceptance.

When your teen is applying to colleges, they'll need your student's GPA. They might ask for the class rank as well. Even if your teen is in an unranked school system, colleges can figure out where your child would be in the school's rank. Colleges can use a student's GPA and compare it to other students with same GPA and size of student body. This will give them a general idea of where your child would rank.

It's important for your teen to learn how to study when they're younger! Don't let him or her wait until high school "when it counts" because they won't know what they're doing.

Heads up, even if your child got all As in middle school, high school is a totally different story. College will be even harder.

Colleges do like to see AP classes on your child's transcript. However, it isn't the only thing that they're looking for. If your child is stressing to much about this, then maybe take one a semester, or even just one a year.

If they're worried that isn't enough, this would be a good question for the college. If it will affect their grades negatively because they're too stressed out to do well, then I'd advise against.

My oldest son took one AP class his senior year. That was it–one, total! He still got accepted to all six colleges that he applied to. Your teen needs to enjoy the teenage years, so these classes need to be carefully considered.

Encourage your teen to take a study-skills class.

Tell him or her to blame it on you if your teen's friends ask why he or she is taking the "dummy" class. This was a crazy misconception that some of my son's friends had, and they teased him about it! He says that the class has helped him so much in school!

Study skills is really a class for smart people who want to know how to get ahead. This class will help them to learn how to study, be organized, and learn what it is that teachers are looking for. This will be a *huge* step ahead for your child.

Some students are naturally organized and quickly figure out how to study. Don't assume that your child is one of these people. If he or she takes this class and realizes it's already something they know, then it will be an easy A. Better to take the class and get some good ideas than not take it and suffer from bad grades in the future.

If there's no such class offered at their middle school or high school, then see if you can find one online or look into a learning center nearby. It will be worth the investment in your child's future.

Another idea: My other son took a speed-reading class because although he's a great reader, he was a slow reader. He took it the summer before his senior year in high school. According to him, it has saved him so much study time since then.

Your child needs to realize that school is his or her most important job at this point.

While they aren't being paid to go to school, good grades will pay off later in school acceptance and money available to them in the form of scholarships.

Getting into the habit of good study skills and work completion when your teen is younger will make school so much easier. This will make the transition into high school much smoother.

Every hour **in** school should equal **at least** a half hour of studying—the night after class, the next night, during study hall, over the weekend, or all of the above. By high school, you can figure that there will be four to five classes with homework in a given day. That would equal to a couple of hours of homework a night minimum.

School is the priority right now. Your teen should use study hall to get homework-type items finished. That way, the time at home can be used to study. There is a difference in those two words, homework and study. Your teen needs to learn what they both mean, and do them regularly.

Homework is doing schoolwork outside of the classroom, as in worksheets, writing papers, and so on. Studying is reading, rereading, taking notes, and synthesizing information given in class and assignments. It's interacting with the information given by the teacher and the work assigned. Studying would also include prepping for tests and quizzes.

There is a disagreement about whether or not students should even have a study hall. I think this is because if kids take a study hall, then they're losing out on a taking another class for credit.

My boys both say yes to study hall. I agree. They both had a study hall almost every semester in high school with a block schedule. They used the time to do homework and study. When they were on sports teams or in a play or whatever, they were so glad to have this extra time. They still got into college.

Colleges look at GPA, test scores, and classes taken. I don't know for sure if they even look at gaps in kid's schedules for study hall—do they have time to do that?

Here's a secret that no one really tells you.

When your senior is applying to colleges, which is the fall of senior year, colleges only ask for grades up to the end of junior year. This means that those first three years of high school are extremely important for the GPA.

Of course, your teen can continue to update his or her grades to send to schools, but early acceptance can be determined by the grades just up to this point.

You have now been made aware.

One thing to remember is that most schools offer financial aid packages in tiers. Grades are **one** thing a tier is based on. The higher the GPA, the better financial package your teen will receive from the schools he or she is interested in, so grades do matter.

This is where you will get the bulk of financial aid for your child—from the college they attend. So your teen needs to focus on grades and test scores.

10

CONVERSATION #7

ACT AND SAT SCORES

Conversation #7 isn't a surprise to most parents. There is some information, though, that might help you to decide how many times your child should take a certain test. You'll also find out why these scores are so important.

Do these tests scores matter? In a word, yes.

Which of these tests does your teen's college of choice require?

If their favorite college only requires one of these tests, then focus on that one. If it's a choice, then your teens should take each test once and see how they do on each. If they do really well on one, then they should stick with that score. Or even better, study to see if they can do better.

Test scores are the other item that determines tiers of financial aid at colleges. The higher the test score, the more money your teen will receive. A perfect score can mean a full ride! These scores are important!

A counselor at one testing center told me that for **every** point improved on the ACT over the schools lowest required point value, it meant the difference of $1,000 per year in tuition. That's a **minimum** $4,000 swing on a test score!

Let's say a student scored a 27 on the ACT and qualified for $5,000 off her tuition each year at a certain college. She retook the test and scored a 28. That could mean she now would receive $6,000 off her tuition each year instead. That's a total difference of $4,000. It could be a bigger (or smaller) swing, but once over the school's minimum score, it will mean more money for your student.

Your child should be prepared.

Your teen should study as much as he or she can before each test to improve his or her score. There are classes for test-taking offered online and at high schools. Many times, the classes at school are offered for free or a very small fee. There are learning centers that also offer these classes.

Your teen can **buy** a book specific to the test or **borrow** from the library or a friend. A good friend of mine told me she would pick up a study guide at a bookstore and drink coffee right there in the store while she studied and took notes out of the book for free. She was in high school, and her parents couldn't afford for her to take a study class for the ACT. No one ever said anything to her! She ended up getting a 31, which is a great score!

Your child should try to get the best score that they can. They can study, take practice tests, and maybe a test prep class. However, with the current scandals in the news, everyone needs to remember that college isn't the only option. There's no stigma to community college, trade schools, the military or just plain getting a job to figure some things out.

Keep in mind that this score isn't the end-all, be-all! My son was accepted to all six schools that he applied to when his ACT score was still a 24. That isn't a terrible score, but it could have been much higher. His score improved on a later test, and his package from the college of his choice is amazing. He still scored below a 30.

Don't let finances stop you from taking these tests.

If finances are preventing your teen from taking these tests, have them talk with their guidance counselor. In the state of Missouri, all juniors are given the ACT at no cost. Find out if there's a program in your state or even the school district that could help if this's a problem.

To be clear, these tests are providing information to colleges about the knowledge base of your student. Unfortunately, they're also an indication of how well your child handles a test situation.

Our other son did not do well on the ACT. He tried three different times and took two classes for improving his score. The classes didn't help. There was one college that he couldn't get into because of this low test score.

He's doing well in college now, but these colleges have to draw the line somewhere for awarding financial aid. There are always other options for college or elsewhere!

CONVERSATION #8

EXTRACURRICULAR ACTIVITIES

Conversation #8 is all about fun stuff. Clubs, activities, sports, and so on are what high school is all about. Your child should take advantage of all the opportunities.

Research has shown that the more involved students are, the more successful they'll be later. Involvement also reduces the chances of dropping out. It's a great way to meet and make friends too.

Throughout your child's time in high school, no matter what their future holds, they'll need a well-rounded resume! This means they need to get involved with **some** extracurricular activities. There are many ways to do this, but they need to remember not to get overinvolved.

Well-rounded means an assortment of activities.

This includes both school and community. It means some leadership positions. It means trying a sport—your child doesn't need to get a varsity letter, just participate.

Get a job. Play an instrument in the school band or a garage band. Get published. Volunteer at school, at church, in the community.

Your teen doesn't have to do **all** these things. They should pick a few things they find interesting, and then join a club or two. There are many activities to choose from once they're in high school.

Colleges and future bosses are looking for participation, "stick-to-itiveness," and leadership.

Your teens don't need to be president of everything. Choosing one club that's their passion is great. They don't even have to be president to show leadership, maybe just lead an event within that particular club.

If they're in any other clubs, participation isn't enough. They should try to stay involved for at least two years. Otherwise, their resume looks choppy and like they can't stick with anything.

Your teen should be ready to discuss their activities. Colleges will have interview questions about the things listed on the resume from high school. Extracurricular activities are great topics for college interviews.

Keep track of everything.

Anytime your teens do anything, they need to take a picture of the event or get a signature. They should keep a journal of activities for each year of high school. Your child should begin keeping track of activities and honors in middle school. This will help them to get into this habit.

Here's a great way that you, as a parent, can help. Keep track of dates and times. Print off a certificate that shows participation. This should include information for all activities. Keep awards, emails, and certificates in a file.

Also, it's good practice for your teens to get the contact information for any adult involved in their lives. Whether it's their bosses at their part-time job or teachers or sponsors of a club, they should get both an email and phone number.

This will help in case the information is needed on an application for school, a job or a scholarship. This information will also be needed to write a resume.

Cocurricular may be a new term for you.

It's another word for *service*. It's a term for anything learned outside the regular curriculum in the community. There needs to be some sort of service activity on your teen's resume!

Service can be many things. Working at a local food bank. Teaching Sunday school. Helping with a fundraiser. Even better would be organizing and leading the event.

Babysitting wouldn't usually count because your teen would normally do this for money. But with that being said, if your child is helping out by babysitting siblings because of an unusual situation occurring in your home, then it might count if they were to describe that circumstance on an application or resume.

Anything that provides a service for someone should count.

Just one club or sport could make a difference in your child's high school experience. My husband and I asked that our boys each join at least one club and try one sport. Note that we said try—we did not expect them to letter or start on a team.

Our oldest son, who isn't athletic, ended up trying out for track and making it! He participated for a couple of years and really enjoyed it. He was in the drama club, and acted in a number of the school plays. He also participated in DECA (a leadership and personal development organization for marketing students) for his business classes, which he really liked as well.

The middle son played baseball until his senior year when he was injured. He also joined DECA, and loved his Young Life group. The latter wasn't a school-sponsored activity, but it still counted as a club on his resume.

Fun and participation are the main goals. Set a minimum expectation and see where it takes your teen. Our boys enjoyed their years of high school, and we think that these clubs and activities helped.

12

CONVERSATION #9

GET TO KNOW THE TEACHERS

Conversation #9 is important. The people who teach our kids are amazing. Are they perfect? No, but they teach because they like kids. They want to affect our kids' lives for the better. They want to be there for our teens.

Our kids should spend time with these amazing adults who want to help them get ahead. Teachers can become mentors and provide much-needed advice to our teens in a way that we, as parents, cannot.

Teens should use their time in high school to build rapport with teachers. It's hard during class to really get to know a teacher. Encourage your teen to talk to teachers during clubs and activities and learn more about them as regular people. Bonus: they'll have these teachers as friends.

High school can be a really fun time, but it's also stressful.

Your teens are trying to grow up, form opinions, do homework, and possibly have a part-time job as well as deal with parents, siblings, and other real-life issues. They'll need to lean on these teachers who were put into their lives for a reason.

Teachers are used to all the teenage issues. Their teachers might have a story of teens in similar situations. All the things that your teens experience are new to them, but probably not new to the teacher. Encourage your teens to talk with their teachers.

These teachers also need to get to know your teen!

Encourage your teen to foster relationships with teachers and coaches. Teens need to keep in mind that they might be asking these same people to write a letter of recommendation someday soon. Or they may be asking teachers to put them up toward some sort of academic or extracurricular event such as boys' state or a DECA team. Tell your teen to show their teachers that they're hardworking and respectful.

Parents should also try to meet the teachers at least once during the school year. There is often a back-to-school night for parents. My boys knew that my husband and I would always go to this. They didn't choose to come with us, but that was fine. We just wanted to put a face to each name. Try to meet their counselor as well.

School counselors are also great resources.

Most school counselors, like the teachers, are struggling under a giant workload. However, they're just like teachers in that they're there to help your teen. Encourage your students to go meet with their counselors by the end of their first semesters of high school. My boys had a great counselor, and I know it helped her to put a name with each of their faces.

Be patient. If you or your teens need something from the counselors, remember that the counselors are serving hundreds of other students and have deadlines of their own. Give the counselor plenty of time when you're requesting anything from a meeting to a class change to a letter of recommendation.

Remember: the counselors can help with scholarship searches, college planning, and schedule changes. Counselors are great resources for your teens during these crazy, busy years.

Each of our older boys had a number of special teachers in high school. They were able to store their lunches in the teacher's rooms. Or go to their classrooms for a break from their friends. Or help them with their classes for service hours. Each of these special teachers provided safe and friendly places for them during the day.

These teachers wrote wonderful letters of recommendation for my boys' college applications and their Boy Scout Eagle requirements. My boys still keep in touch with a handful of these wonderful people who made such positive impacts on their lives.

13

CONVERSATION #10

LETTERS OF RECOMMENDATION

Conversation #10 goes hand in hand with the previous conversation. Teachers as well as other adults will need to be asked for letters of recommendation. Make sure that asking for these is something that your teen feels comfortable doing. It's politer to ask in person, but an email is very common as well.

Most colleges will require letters of recommendation. Many future bosses will require them. Many times a school will require two to three teacher or guidance counselor recommendations, one or two from community persons, and one from a pastor or scout leader. Many schools require three to five total. This is also true for scholarship applications as well.

Here are some rules to remember when asking for a letter of recommendation.

When your teen is asking for a letter of recommendation, be sure they're specific about what the recommendation is for. Is it for a college application? Is it for a scholarship? Is it for a job? Read the fine print carefully with your student, and be sure that he or she convey this information completely when asking an adult for the recommendation.

Your teen should ask for the recommendation a good two to three weeks in advance of the actual due date so that there's **no** worry of it being late.

About a week before the recommendation is due, your teen should send a thank-you email to the writer. This is both courteous and a good trick to put the recommendation back in the front of the mind of a very busy person. A handwritten thank-you note after the fact is a nice touch and a courteous way to convey appreciation.

Have your teen give the writer the link to the particular website or print out what the particulars are for each scholarship.

Give the writer the option to say no.

Your student should leave himself plenty of time to find someone else. In fact, your teen should have a list of possible adults that they know and would be comfortable asking.

Most adults will say yes. If they say no, your teen shouldn't feel discouraged. It's most likely because they have something else going on that prevents them from being able to help. Your teen needs to ask early in case his or her first choice of a writer has to say no.

Send a thank-you note!

After the recommendation has been received from the letter writer, your teen should send a thank-you note to them as soon as possible. This person did a very nice thing, and your child should definitely show his or her appreciation!

If your teen isn't that comfortable talking with other adults, then it's time to start practicing. Maybe do some roleplaying with adults who are familiar to them. Looking someone in the eye and having a firm handshake are two soft skills that your teen needs to have as he or she moves into the adult world.

❧ 14 ❧

CONVERSATION #11

CONTACT AND VISIT COLLEGES

Conversation #11 is a fun one. Read on to learn more.

I read somewhere that colleges keep track of the number of times that you contact them.

I think this is true based on my own son's experience with a small, elite private college out east.

Our oldest son contacted a college that he'd read about toward the end of his eighth-grade year. In that first email, he introduced himself and told them where he'd heard of the college. He asked a few questions about the campus and other things that interested him. He kept in touch and formed a bond with the admissions counselor assigned to the Midwest.

We visited the school during spring break of his junior year. It was an amazing college. They tried really hard to get him to come to their school. The college sent many different items through the mail over time, such as a key chain, bumper sticker, and a hat. They also sent numerous letters and emails.

He was really torn when trying to make a decision his senior year. The college continued to throw more and more scholarship money at him, knowing that the expense and cost of travel was a real drawback affecting his decision. His final decision was to go somewhere closer to home. He let them know of this.

He finally had to ask them to stop contacting him. I think it made a big difference to them that he initiated the contact and had fostered a good relationship with them for the next four years.

He had continued to reach out anytime that he had a question about their school. He sent his grades each semester after his freshman year. Each time he contacted the school, they reached back out to him. They had built a relationship, and I know that this college was disappointed he chose another school because they told him.

How should your teen express interest?

Find the website for a college that's of interest to your teen. Look for the admissions tab. Send off for the basic admissions packet. If possible, do this before senior year. If your child is really interested in a college, have him or her do this in middle school, the earlier the better. You never know! I know that the relationship that my son built with his initial number one choice was instrumental in the amount of money they offered. He did have a great resume, but that relationship built a bond, and they really wanted him at their school.

Have your teen write a letter to the college letting them know that they are your teen's dream school and give them **specific** reasons why. Your child should continue contacting the school over time with questions that might come up. He or she should send the child's resume as it evolves over time. The middle of junior year is a good time.

By the time your teen is a junior, the school will send an updated packet of information. This will happen because your child will be in their system from their previous communication. At this time, your teen can let the college know that their interests have changed or let them know that they're still interested.

Visit colleges your teen is interested in!

If possible, visit colleges during the school year. That way your teen can get a clear picture of what the campus is like during a normal school day. Set up an interview with the admissions staff before the visit.

Be early or, even better, on time. Ask for a school tour. Interviews and tours can be set up online ahead of time. Most colleges will treat your family to a lunch on campus.

Remember: They're showing off for you. If the school doesn't offer meal tickets, then ask where there is a good place to eat on campus. I bet you they give you a meal ticket.

Your teen should be an active participant in the interview.

Have your teen be ready with their own questions for the interview. Ask questions about classes, majors, working on campus, and scholarships that might be available. Ask about housing, extracurricular activities, alumni base, job placement at graduation. The college should cover most of those topics anyway, but definitely have questions ready.

Parents, let your teen lead the way with the conversation. If you have a question or two, that's fine, but you shouldn't be the one taking charge. This is the time for your teen to shine. You want him or her to be the one with the answers and not looking to you for help. The school is interviewing your teen, not you.

Talk with your teen ahead of time and agree on some questions that you'll each ask. Write down the questions if that helps your teen to be more comfortable. This is supposed to be a two-way conversation between the college and your child.

Sometimes, there will be an actual one-on-one interview with just your teen and an admissions officer, so your teen should be ready for that possibility.

Plan an overnight stay on the campus for your teen.

Most schools schedule overnight visits regularly, and they pick fun, outgoing students to host prospective students. It will give your child a feel for life on campus. My son did this at a couple of schools, and he really enjoyed the experience of being a "college kid" for a night.

Encourage your teen to have an open mind when looking for a college.

Look at big and small schools. Look at public and private. Try to look at one that's a little further away from home than they might want. Your teen will never know what might be a good fit until they're able to compare different campuses.

One last thing, do **not** rule out the private schools! In today's economy, leave no stone unturned. This was a total surprise to us. Private schools are very competitive and can honor a strong resume, good grades, and so on with money.

The financial package our son received from the small private school he's attending beat the local state school by many thousands of dollars! In fact, all the private schools he applied to were able to award money for things like his Eagle, boys' state, and other interesting things that he was able to put on his resume.

Encourage your teen to reach out to a college at some point in either middle school or high school. It can be a really fun and rewarding experience in many ways.

CONVERSATION #12

WRITING THE COLLEGE ESSAY

Conversation #12 gets into the nitty-gritty of actually applying to colleges. Have your teen try some of these tips, especially if they aren't a great writer. Practice makes perfect!

There are many books and websites that will help your teen to write college essays. I won't try to tell you how to write an essay here. What I will do is encourage your teen to start writing a few essays **now** to practice. Like any art, it needs to be practiced.

There are an infinite number of topics to write about.

Most college or scholarship applications require an essay. Many times, the college will give the student a specific topic. The trick is to be ready.

As your family begins searching for colleges, look at what the colleges need on their applications. As your student begins searching for scholarships, look at the topics they ask you to write about.

There are many common themes, for instance, "Describe your future plans." This could include the choice of a major or where your teen wants to go to college or what are their plans for after college. Writing an essay on future plans (at this time) is a great start. This can be tweaked to fit different circumstances later.

Another popular topic is "Safe Driving: Don't Text and Drive". Another one is "What Can Be Done to Save the Environment?" Another, "Our American Constitution." One more is "Describe a Life-Changing Experience." These are all topics that I've seen over and over the past few years as I have helped my boys search for essay topics and scholarships.

The idea is to write four to five basic essays, and then tweak them to fit different situations later as opportunities arrive. Your teen needs to personalize each one when actually submitting them. This means to take the topic, and the particular scholarship and put them together in a way that's original, even though the subject matter may already be mostly written.

The goal is to stand out from all the other essays being submitted.

Start with a great opening sentence, the "hook," and include interesting supporting details. Write a conclusion that fits with the rest of the essay and makes it personalize it somehow.

If writing isn't your child's strength, then get her help!

Your teens can ask their English teachers. Or they should ask others adult in their lives who are known to be good writers. They can ask tutors who could be professionals, classmate, or anyone with solid knowledge of essay writing. Many people would be willing to help, but your child just shouldn't wait until the last minute.

Your teen should have some ideas jotted down, maybe even a rough draft. If your teen has a passion about something, then they can write an essay about that to add to their arsenal.

Save all essays in Word or Google.docs. This will be helpful later so that they can just cut and paste and edit as needed.

One more tip would be to Google the past few year's Common App essay topics. This will give your teen a good idea of what to expect. (The Common App is used by many colleges as a way to apply to their school. It's one application that can be used for many colleges.)

Writing is a part of life, whether your child goes to college or not. The ability to get thoughts onto paper is a lifelong skill. Your teen may not have to write essays after all their schooling, but they'll always need to be able to express themselves. The written word is used in almost every job.

❧ 16 ❧

CONVERSATION #13

RESPECT THE LAW AND OTHER RULES

Conversation #13 seems like common sense, but read on to be able to remind your teen about a few things.

Rule followers are often referred to as "nerds" or "brown nosers," but the fact is that laws are in place to keep teens safe and to protect them. This includes laws such as driving restrictions and town curfews, but also rules that are in place at school and at home.

Rules are developed over time for many reasons.

Your teen might not see the need for certain rules to be in place, but there's a time and a place for trying to get things changed. (High school would be a tricky time for this, so encourage your teen to proceed cautiously.)

Be on time. Be early if possible. Tardiness is a bad habit. Most schools have a rule regarding this. This isn't a difficult rule to follow. Teachers and bosses will love your teens for being prompt.

Turn in all work. Neatly, completed, and on time. No excuses. Even if your teen gets a bad grade, all the aforementioned attributes will go a long way toward a better discussion with the teacher later if need be.

Turn off their phones. Most teachers have policies regarding use of technology. Your teens need to follow their rules! If there is an extenuating circumstance, they should explain what the problem is. Most of the time, teachers are going to be more willing to work with your teen if there have been no problems in the past. This is true about most situations.

Another time to be off of their phones is in the car when driving, enough said.

Beware of social media. *Everything* your teen puts online or texts or tweets or snaps is out in cyberspace *forever*. It seems as if it can be deleted, and in most instances, it does disappear. But there's a way to trace all these things even if seemingly "deleted."

Scholarships and jobs have been lost and relationships ended or at least forever altered over information that's found online. Only post positive and appropriate things. Or don't post, period.

Finally, be respectful. Teachers are working in the classroom 99 percent of the time because they really like kids. Believe me: they're *not* doing it for the money. They have lives of their own. Kids of their own. Problems of their own.

Your teen shouldn't cause the teacher any problems. If your child has an issue, he or she should bring it up outside of class. Your teen might be surprised by how much the teacher is willing to help. If there's a conflict that absolutely cannot be avoided, your teen should still be respectful.

Most of this conversation is common sense to us. Many of our teens need to be reminded of all these things on occasion. This conversation can be revisited many times. I know in our house the number of times probably can't be counted. As situations occur, use them as tools to reinforce the talking points above.

Someone is watching at all times.

There have been many instances where bad behavior has affected college acceptance, getting into a club, keeping a job, or even just getting an interview. Social media is everywhere, and your teen needs to know that colleges and future employers will be checking.

This means that it's best to stay out of trouble because no matter where your teen goes, someone will have a phone and record the incident. He or she needs to make good choices at all times.

Teachers will be watching and listening in the halls, in classes, and during clubs and sporting events. Tell your teen to let them see and hear good things.

CONVERSATION #14

SCHOLARSHIP SEARCH

Conversation #14 is a big one. With this information, your teen can save themselves and your family money. You and your teen need to know that they can apply for scholarships all the way through college. The more that your child applies for, the more success he or she will have. Your child should never stop trying!

Did you know that your teen can apply for scholarships at the age of thirteen?

It's true. There are a number of websites that offer different scholarships and sweepstakes for ages thirteen though college. Look at Fastweb.com, Cappex.com, and Schoolguidance.com for more information. You can also look at Scholly.com, Chegg.com, ScholarshipOwl.com and Niche.com. These are just a few.

The great thing is that both you and your teen can create a different login for each site. Each of you will need to fill out the information asked based on your teen's interests.

You will both receive emails from the sites. This is a great way for parents to help.

When my kids are busy, I can screen the offers and forward the ones that I think they might be interested in to their email. The boys just delete the ones that they don't want to work on or aren't interested in. I can also remind them monthly to reenter the sweepstakes that are available.

One thing to think about—both you and your teen should set up email accounts that are **just** for the scholarship search.

Otherwise, your regular email address will be swamped. Do **not** sign up for all the scholarship websites.

Look at them all and choose one or two. They all send a lot of emails, so be particular. You can always opt out later if it's too much.

Another good place to look for scholarships is the school guidance office. Even in middle school. Have your teens tell their guidance counselors what colleges they're interested in, and which classes they enjoy. They can steer your teens toward opportunities as they become available.

Keep in mind that not a lot of students like to put forth much effort into these opportunities. So, sometimes, luckily for your teen, there isn't much competition!

One thing to remember is that usually only one scholarship will be earned for every six to ten that are applied for. (road2college.com) This means to start early and consistently keep trying. Be sure to read all the fine print and turn in everything that's required. Don't waste your time on the sweepstakes.

Scholarships can also be found in places of business (banks, insurance companies, and investment companies to name a few) and on company websites. Look for a scholarship tab on websites. You might be surprised at the places that you will find scholarships.

MY HUSBAND MADE AN ANALOGY THAT OUR BOYS understood.

He asked the boys if they'd go dig a hole in the yard if he paid them $8 an hour. They said yes, but they really didn't want to.

He told them, the size of the hole would take about two hours, so they would each receive $16. Would they be willing to do this? Again, reluctantly, they said yes.

Compare that to filling out an application and maybe spending an hour or two on an essay for up to $500, $1,000, or maybe even more. Would they be willing to do that? Of course, they couldn't say no!

Not trying for any scholarships is like throwing money away. At no other time in your teens' lives will there be money basically being thrown at them for not a whole lot of effort on their parts.

Sometimes it will be just a questionnaire, sometimes an

essay, sometimes filling out an application, sometimes a combination of these things.

Encourage your teen to take some time to apply for at least a few, maybe even just one a month. It could make a huge difference!

Our oldest son has applied for and won scholarships offered by his fraternity. He has applied two years in a row, and has gotten money both times. Those, plus an amount he received from them for grades his freshman year, have totalled to about three thousand dollars!

All three boys have tried for different scholarships over the years, but that's the only amount they've received. But I always encourage them to keep trying because if they don't try, then for sure they won't get any amount.

❧ 18 ❧
FINAL THOUGHTS

College isn't the only option out there.

Have an open mind if your child thinks that college isn't part of their future. Many great careers aren't dependent on college. I have researched some great choices for those teens who think that college isn't the path they would like to follow.

Here are a few other choices: welder, HVAC, lineman, electrician, sonographer, paralegal, construction worker, barber or beautician, lpn, plumber, automotive technician, or trucker. This is just the start of a very long list.

The nice thing about many of these jobs is that the training or schooling required for many of them is two years or less. Some of these trades can be learned by apprenticing, which can mean learning while working *and* getting paid right out of high school. The demand for these skills is extremely high as well.

For instance, HVAC tech jobs are predicted to increase at a rate of 15 percent through 2026, according to the Bureau of Labor Statistics (BLS). This is more than twice as fast as the national average for *all* occupations! The BLS also states that the need for welders is expected to grow by 26 percent by 2020.

Almost all those skilled jobs listed above, as well as many more not listed, have growth rates of 12 percent or more, which is higher than the general growth rate of employment of 7 percent.

The kids who go these routes will most likely start their working lives much earlier than their cohorts who opt for four-year college. Therefore, they'll make money much sooner. They may have to get loans for trade school. However, the loans aren't as high as for a typical college degree.

Once the kids who go through college pay back their student loans (average loan amount is $37,000), they have the potential to make more in the long run than the skilled workers. This is because skilled workers are just that—trained in one skill. This means less flexibility in the future.

However, if these future skilled workers decide to continue their education, then they'll have more flexibility as well. This is important because average workers today change jobs/careers three times during their lifetimes. This is all according to *Two Cents* on PBS.

I wrote this book because I want to help others going through this season of life.

Start these conversations and see where they lead you. Do your research, and guide your teens through these crazy years called high school.

It's an exciting, yet daunting process to help your "almost adult" child make lifelong decisions.

There are so many books and articles about potty training, toddler temper tantrums, and getting ready for kindergarten.

It seemed as if the resources for parenting teens were available, but just so scattered and hard to find when our oldest son became a teenager. I wanted to pass along what we had learned and also the strategy that has worked best for us.

Conversations were the *key* to all of this working.

Start these talks as soon as you can. It's really fun to watch how your child grows up and makes decisions and then moves on and out. Use a notebook for each child from the beginning! We didn't really do this until we started needing to keep track of things from conversation to conversation.

Some conversations will go great. Others will be very frustrating for everyone involved. Don't give up. Just decide to talk another day. Even if nothing was really accomplished in one particular conversation. That's okay!

Your kids need to know that you're there and that you care. This process is proof positive that you're doing both of those things.

This whole process was a little scary at first because my husband and I hadn't done anything like this before, and there was so much for us to learn as parents. Now some of these conversations just evolve as we're hanging out with our kids. I don't even realize that we're making headway until all of a sudden a decision is made!

We prayed a lot, spent time on the computer searching for answers, read a lot, asked more questions, and prayed some more. We talked with our kids **and** each other.

We have gotten two children through high school and into college successfully. Our boys had a great time in high school, and they learned a lot.

They each made different decisions about college, and so far they're doing well. The boys are as different as they could be, but our conversation system worked with both of them.

We visited a lot of schools, which seemed excessive at the time, but I was grateful for the time I got to spend with each of my boys. The discussions we had before, during and after we visited each school were priceless. We learned a lot throughout this process. We have one more boy to go, and I feel as if we know more about the process for the final go around.

I know that some things will change before our eighth

grader reaches his senior year. We'll be ready for whatever comes his way because he has been and will continue to be part of many conversations just like his brothers before him.

Good luck to you!

SELF-PUBLISHING
SCHOOL

NOW IT'S YOUR TURN

Discover the EXACT 3-step blueprint you need to become a bestselling author in 3 months.

Self-Publishing School helped me, and now I want them to help you with this FREE WEBINAR!

Even if you're busy, bad at writing, or don't know where to start, you CAN write a bestseller and build your best life.

With tools and experience across a variety of niches and professions, Self-Publishing School is the only resource you need to take your book to the finish line!

DON'T WAIT

Watch this FREE WEBINAR now, and
Say "YES" to becoming a bestseller:

[Watch Now!]

CAN YOU HELP?

Yes, please!

Thank You For Reading My Book!

I really appreciate all of your feedback, and I love hearing what you have to say.

I need your input to make the next version of this book and my future books better.

Please leave me an honest review on Amazon letting me
know what you thought of the book.

Also, visit our website
www.parentinghighschoolers.com
for some tips and tools to use along with this book!

Thanks so much!

Melanie Studer

ABOUT THE AUTHOR

Melanie Studer has a BS in Education with two decades of parenting and classroom experience. She has worked with students preschool through high school. Her oldest two sons are in college now. She is passionate about helping families to know their options and keeping the lines of parent/child communication open. She encourages students to expand their world through service, leadership and volunteering–"a well-rounded student makes a better citizen."

Mel is a wife and mom of three boys and two dogs. She is a lover of reading, teaching, and writing. She blogs for parents of teens at:

www.parentinghighschoolers.com

Made in the USA
Las Vegas, NV
19 January 2021

16186669R00065